D0743276

Kansas Impressions

Marguerite — 1973

A Christmas to remember
with love from
Mariam + Les Fleming

Kansas Impressions
PHOTOGRAPHS and WORDS

Photographs by Wes Lyle
Quotations selected by James Fisher

THE UNIVERSITY PRESS OF KANSAS
Lawrence / Manhattan / Wichita

For my wife, Sally,
and in memory of
my mother

Wes Lyle

Publisher's Preface

This is a book of discovery—an exploration of Kansas in photographs and words. The photographs are by Wes Lyle, and they are matched with quotations researched by James Fisher. The maps provide an accurate sense of place for each photograph.

The following geographical and geological description of Kansas is excerpted from *Kansas Wild Flowers,* by William Chase Stevens:

Kansas is a prairie state because its annual precipitation is sufficient to sustain grasses but not for forests to prevail, excepting along streams and seepage and drainage places of slopes and draws.

Owing to diminishing precipitation and increasing evaporative power of the air from east to west, vegetation is sorted into three zones of longitude: on the east, the tall-grass prairie, or true prairie; on the west, the short-grass plains; the mixed prairie of associated tall grasses and short grasses between the first two zones.

Kansas is predominantly an undulating plain sloping gently downward towards the east on an average of about 10-15 feet per mile, from an elevation above sea level of 3500-3900 feet (locally 4135 feet in Wallace County) along the west border to less than 750 feet on the east border. Also a dip towards the southeast along the south half of the state is shown by the course of the streams, the lowest elevation of less than 700 feet occurring in Montgomery County where the Verdigris River crosses the border into Oklahoma.

The surface features and vertical structure of the state are the result of physical processes through an inconceivably long period of time. . . .

The state is divided into eight physiographic regions according to surface configuration and geological structure, as follows:

Cherokee Lowland (southeast); Mississippian and Pennsylvanian limestone, sandstone, and shale. This region surpasses all other parts of the state in the production of coal; and zinc and lead are mined in southeast Cherokee County, where Mississippian limestone is at or near the surface. The land is level to gently rolling. The soil is mostly residual from the weathering of shale and is low in lime, phosphorus, nitrogen, and organic matter; and large areas are poorly drained. Hardpan occurs from 6 to 18 inches below the surface.

Osage Plains, extending west to Manhattan and Emporia. The region is marked by north-south ranges of hills extending across the width of the state, with east-facing escarpments of hard limestone. Between the ridges the land, worn down to lower levels through softer strata, is flat to gently rolling. Excepting the alluvium of the flood plains of rivers and the

COUNTY MAP OF KANSAS

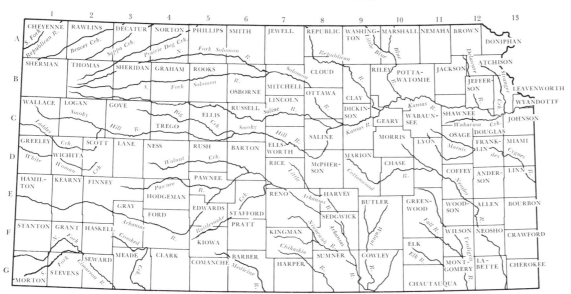

FINDING LIST OF COUNTIES

PHYSIOGRAPHIC MAP OF KANSAS

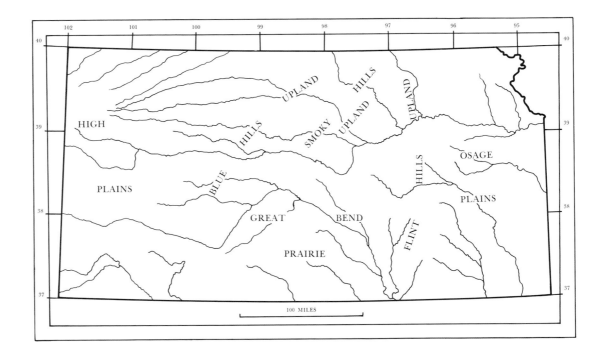

glaciated area east of the Big Blue and north of the Kansas River valley, a large part of the soil is residual from the weathering of Pennsylvanian and Permian limestone, shale, and sandstone strata, the latter local and subordinate in amount but prevailing in parts of Woodson, Wilson, and Montgomery counties, where it yields a soil low in lime, phosphorus, and nitrogen. The soil of the glaciated area is a deposit of transported granite and quartzite rock, local rocks, gravel, sand, and clay (collectively called *till*). Finally, the winds sweeping across this deposit have spread a mantle of dust over the eastern counties and built up the bluffs bordering the Missouri River. Soils laid down by the wind are called *loess* (from German *loesen*, "to loosen"). Hardpan is seldom present in these relatively young soils, and where it is apparent it is still not dense enough to keep roots from growing through it.

Flint Hills Upland. This region extends north-south across the state and west to Arkansas City, Salina, and Clay Center. The dominant feature is the range of Flint Hills with east-facing escarpments of hard limestone, the land between the ridges for the most part gently rolling. The region belongs to the Permian system, and the soil is chiefly residual from the weathering of limestone. The valleys are fertile and suited to general agriculture and the region is famed for its vast expanse of bluestem pastures.

Smoky Hills Upland. Cretaceous formation, extending from the northern border of the state to the Arkansas River. The surface is gently rolling between the hills, which have east-facing sandstone escarpments. The soil is residual, principally from the weathering of Dakota sandstone.

Blue Hills Upland. Cretaceous formation, characterized by many long spurs, with hard limestone escarpments, forming the divides between east-flowing streams. The soil is residual from the weathering of limestone, chalk, and shale. The soil as a rule is rather deep and fertile and hardpan is but little developed.

High Plains. Tertiary and Quaternary formations principally, extending across the width and about one-third the length of the state. The plains descend from about 4000 feet on the west boundary to about 2000 feet at the east margin of the region near Ellis County. Across a large part of this region a thick deposit of wind-borne silt has been laid down over inwash sand, gravel, and clay from Colorado. The surface for the most part is flat or gently rolling and in the north half broken by the valleys of east- and northeast-flowing streams and their tributaries. Some of the streams have excavated their valleys through the Tertiary and deep into the chalk and chalky shale of the Cretaceous. This is strikingly exhibited along the valley of the Smoky Hill River through Trego, Gove, and Logan counties. South of the Smoky Hill River and its tributaries the surface is relatively unbroken as far as the Arkansas River, where there are bluffs north of the river and sand hills south of it from the Colorado line eastward into Ford County. Beyond the river to the south border the soil is inwash material from Colorado but is mixed with relatively infertile plains marl (a composition of clay and lime) locally where stream erosion has reduced the inwash cover. A unique feature of the High Plains is the broad bed of an ancient lake between the towns Meade and Fowler in Meade County, lying below the general level and now in wet weather the site of many ponds. In general it may be said of the broad expanse of the High Plains that the soil is deep and fertile and requires but a moderate precipitation to insure high productivity.

Great Bend Prairie, extending east from the 75-mile northeast trend of the Arkansas River to the beginning of the Flint Hills Upland, and southeast to some distance south of Wichita. The region is a flat to gently rolling plain with sand dunes and sand hills bordering the river and sporadically at some distance from it. The soils are chiefly loam and sandy loam from fine outwash and wind deposits of the Tertiary and Quaternary formations, but residual soils from the weathering of Permian limestone and shale predominate in the southeast section. As a whole the soils are fertile, adapted to general farming, and especially productive of winter wheat.

Red Hills Upland or *Cimarron Breaks,* south and west of the Great Bend Prairie. Here the southward-flowing tributaries of the Cimarron and Medicine Lodge rivers have deeply eroded the red sandstone and shale of the Permian age. Much of the broken land is good for grazing, and other areas of this region are productive of winter wheat especially but also of oats, barley, and the sorghums, and a variety of other crops.

Acknowledgments

For their encouragement and assistance in many ways, we are indebted to Paul Miner, John Chandley, Donald T. Jones, and Thorpe Menn, all executives of the *Kansas City Star*.

A special thank you to Yvonne Willingham, University Press of Kansas, for her efforts.

During the many months this project was under way, there were many people in Kansas—far too many to name here—who offered their help; and we wish to thank them, too.

Wes Lyle
James Fisher

Kansas Impressions

This flower has to all Kansans a historic symbolism which speaks of
frontier days, winding trails, pathless prairies, and is full of the
life and glory of the past, the pride of the present, and
richly emblematic of the majesty of a golden future. . . . The . . .
wild native sunflower is hereby made, designated and declared
to be the state flower and floral emblem of the state of Kansas.

Legislative enactment, 1903

Wild native sunflower

We traveled a good part of the way through the Gypsum Hills and
drank "Gyp" water until most of us had fever sores on our lips.
It was still raining and we were doing no work. . . . At . . . Kiowa
there was a saloon and the boys began to "likker up." At
Medicine Lodge there were several saloons and they "likkered up"
some more. At that time Medicine Lodge was strictly a cow
town. The boys were given the freedom of the city. . . . They ran
horse races on Main Street. At night they built bonfires and
tried to see who could ride his horse nearest to the fire.

J. T. Bokin, cowboy, 1883

Erosion, Gypsum Hills
Comanche County

Gypsum Hills west of Medicine Lodge
Barber County

[Horses] were brought in every spring and herded by cowboys trained to the
throwing lasso. They rounded up a herd of from 50 to 100 horses and ponies,
mostly broncos, branded, but wild and unbroken, and gave us a choice.
When two fine ponies were pointed out, they rode slowly around until they cut
them out of the herd. Then a long run by three or four well-mounted men,
until they were lassoed, bridled, and saddled, and were then counted
broken. They made very tough, serviceable riding horses, but
for weeks they could not be trusted.

> William H. Coffin,
> a Society of Friends settler

Rodeo stock roundup
Chase County

Quarter-horse ranch, northwest of Bazaar
Chase County

Horseshoer
Russell County

Annual horse drive through Cottonwood Falls
Chase County

Trail ride
Wallace County

Fox hunt, Ft. Leavenworth
Leavenworth County

When the *New Lucy* finally docked in Kansas City [in 1857], the passengers were hurried from the vessel just before supper under the impression that they might otherwise be carried on to Leavenworth. Holman and I made our way along the levee past boxes, cartons, and all kinds of merchandise, piled wherever space could be found. Slaves were everywhere. There was a moving mass of wagons, animals, and men. The cracking of ox whips, cries of drivers, and braying of mules all added to the confusion. Facing the wharf were a few brick buildings that served as warehouses and outfitting stations for emigrants. . . . Kansas City became the chief point of departure for all regions farther west.

From *One-Way Ticket to Kansas:*
The Autobiography of Frank M. Stahl,
as told to Margaret Whittemore

Traffic over the Lewis and Clark viaduct, Kansas City
Wyandotte County

Freeway over Kawsmouth, Kansas City
Wyandotte County

James Street, Kansas City
Wyandotte County

The temperature in a few hours had fallen below zero. The storm
[the blizzard of 1886], gaining force hourly, continued
throughout the night, and by morning it might very truthfully
be said the state was frozen solid. . . . But little provision was made
by the average man of that day for wintering his stock; in fact,
because of the scarcity of feed, the animals were generally
turned out to shift for themselves. It was as much as the homesteader could do to provide for his family, meager as their
requirements were. Thus, in the sparsely settled western half of the
state, in such a storm there was almost no chance of life for
stock, and but little for man, except those who had dugouts, and
only then when they were fortunate enough to reach them
before the storm attained its height.

O. P. Byers, from *Collections of the
Kansas State Historical Society,*
1911-1912

Stranded traffic near Concordia
Cloud County

Snow fence
Brown County

Farm, Ten Mile Township
Miami County

Watering stock, northeast of Louisburg
Miami County

Two calves
Barton County

Cattle herd north of Salina
Ottawa County

Loading hay for stranded cattle
Barton County

Operation Haylift dumping hay
Clark County

Willow tree
Wabaunsee County

Out on the western plains where tree growth was largely lacking efforts were early made at forestation. Congress in 1873 passed the "Timber Culture Act," making it possible for a homesteader to pre-empt an additional quarter section of land by the simple expedient of planting forty acres of trees on it. This second tract was known as a "tree claim." This law was later repealed, but it resulted in the planting of millions of trees, many of which still survive in the form of groves and shelter belts. These timber tracts had an esthetic value, besides reducing the destructive effects of wind and preventing soil erosion. Some people contend that trees are loved more in Kansas than elsewhere because they are so much needed there.

Margaret Whittemore,
Historic Kansas: A Centenary Sketchbook

Cottonwood tree on the Cimarron River
Grant County

Farmstead
Gove County

One night we had retired, and were trying to believe that
the thunder was but one of those peculiar menacing volleys
of cloud-artillery that sometimes passed over harmlessly; but
we could not sleep, the roar and roll of thunder was
so alarming. There is no describing lightning on the
Plains. While a storm lasts, there seems to be an incessant
glare. . . . In a letter written to my husband [General
Custer] while the effect of the fright was still fresh on my
mind, I told him "the heavens seemed to shower down fire
upon the earth, and in one minute and a half we counted
twenty-five distinct peals of thunder."
  Mrs. Elizabeth B. Custer, from *Tenting on
  the Plains,* written on the Kansas frontier
  following the Civil War

July cloudburst near Matfield Green
Chase County

The spring of '79 will always be memorable for the devastating
cyclones which started in Texas and moved north through
the Indian Territory into western Kansas. Not one alone terrified
the early settlers who were making their homes on the frontier,
but a succession of tornadoes moved over the country at that time,
leaving destruction and death in their wake; a second and
third gleaning what was left of the scanty possessions of the
already impoverished people.

From a story related by
Judge William R. Smith, of the
Atchison, Topeka & Santa Fe Railroad

Tornado damage in Topeka
Shawnee County

Beaver Spring was the first spring in Kansas showing crude oil on its surface. The Indians would camp there to gather oil by placing their blankets on the surface of the spring, and a few hours later wring out the blankets and secure much oil. They used it for frozen parts, for cuts, sprains, for sores on their ponies, and externally for internal ailments.

From a letter written by Ely Moore, Lawrence

Oil storage tank
Wyandotte County

Oil-field workers
Barber County

Oil derrick
Comanche County

By the fall of 1860 there was scarcely any corn or wheat in the Territory; not six thousand bushels of either in each county. . . . The result was that thirty thousand settlers left the Territory and returned to their friends and to provision in the States. It looked at the time as though the whole country would be depopulated and left a barren and uninhabited waste. Claims, with their improvements, houses, fences &c., were abandoned and stood dreary and alone upon the prairies. Long trains of covered wagons, drawn by lean horses, with woe-begone looking inmates, in mournful procession crossed the Border.

J. N. Holloway, *History of Kansas,* 1868

Abandoned farm house
Barton County

Abandoned farm, Sun City
Barber County

Abandoned school near Eskridge
Wabaunsee County

April 8, 1920 was test flight day. The plane was hauled four miles from downtown to the old Wichita Aircraft Company field, assembled, and first piloted by Matty (E. M. Laird) himself. "It was a tense moment at 5:42 o'clock Thursday afternoon when Laird opened wide the throttle of the first airplane made in Wichita, and the untried ship headed into a light southeast wind," said the Wichita *Beacon*.

Sondra Van Meter,
The E. M. Laird Airplane Company

F-101 landing at McConnell Air Force Base
Sedgwick County

The airframe industry, Wichita
Sedgwick County

As the influx of settlers continued, church and school assumed a larger importance. An arbor was constructed and a revival meeting was held, where cow hands who came to scoff sometimes remained to pray. Under the thundering sound of the minister's voice their thoughts turned to the sins of earlier days. . . . Seeing how much a deep religious faith meant to people who must endure the hardships and vicissitudes of pioneer life, they sometimes sought in religion consolation for their own fast-multiplying troubles.

Edward Everett Dale, from the
Mississippi Valley Historical Review,
June 1937

Friends Church
Cheyenne County

Eisenhower Chapel, Abilene
Dickinson County

Holy Rosary Church, Wea
Miami County

Many of the heathen are dying without religion. What shall we say
of them? Or what will they say of us at the bar of God, that
we withheld the lamp of life from their bewildered feet? O that
Christians who are living at ease in Zion would lay these matters to
heart. O, Lord, can it be true that thousands of heathen are
going to hell daily for want of the Gospel? And we, instead of
sending it to them, give our money for tea, coffee, tobacco, fine
clothes, &c. May the Lord have mercy on us.

Western Christian Advocate,
May 10, 1844

Peyote users, Native American
church, Soldier Creek valley
Jackson County

We obtained . . . the following copy of a registration, kept at Council Grove, by S. M. Hays & Co., from the 24th of April to the 1st of October, 1860: Passing west—men, 3,519; wagons, 2,667; horses, 478; mules, 5,819; working cattle, 22,738; carriages, 61; tons of freight, 6,819. The above includes only those engaged in the freighting business. No account was taken of travelers, emigrants, and men engaged in private business.

Parkville & Grand River Railroad Company
Annual Report, 1860

Railroad depot, Coldwater
Comanche County

Freight train west of Leoti
Wichita County

Wheel of old steam locomotive, Pittsburg
Crawford County

We suppose the Fourth of July orators will wave the eagle in the usual extravagant fashion this year, and tell how every man is an intellectual giant, and a patriot, and a kind father and indulgent husband, but as a matter of fact, that sort of nonsense is becoming a little tiresome. . . . Liberty has been carried so far that many people believe we have too much of it. The striking coal miners who refuse to work, or to permit others to take their places, are one result of too much liberty. Coxey is another result. America is overburdened with nonsense, and the next set of Fourth of July orators ought to tell the exact facts, and give the eagle a rest. Out of our abundance we have made as sad a mess as people of other countries have made of their poverty.

E. W. Howe, from the Atchison *Globe*,
May 25, 1894

Fourth of July, Louisburg
Miami County

I would not seriously regret the total disappearance of the buffalo from our western prairies, in its effect upon the Indians, regarding it rather as a means of hastening their sense of dependence upon the products of the soil and their own labors.

Columbus Delano,
Secretary of the Interior,
in his Annual Report, 1873

Buffalo bull, Winchester
Jefferson County

Buffalo cow and calf
McPherson County

Buffalo herd, Roxbury
McPherson County

Buffalo skull, White Woman Creek
Scott County

The starving wolf and his diminutive companion the
coyote, are ready to take advantage of the first favorable
opportunity of hastening the demise of . . . any
buffalo who may have strayed from the herd.
De B. R. Keim, from
Sheridan's Troopers on the Borders, 1870

Coyote
Johnson County

In our intercourse with Indians it must always be borne in mind
that we are the most powerful party . . . . We are assuming, and I
think with propriety, that our civilization ought to take the
place of their barbarous habits. We therefore claim the right to
control the soil which they occupy, and we assume that it is our duty
to coerce them, if necessary, into the adoption and practice of
our habits and customs.

Report of the Secretary of the Interior,
1872

Indian boy, Hoyt
Jackson County

Indian boy, Kickapoo Reservation
Brown County

Indian girl
Jackson County

Indian boy and dog
Jackson County

Indian ceremonial, Mayetta
Jackson County

The Harper family was plowing a field preparatory to making a potato patch, when [they] . . . accidentally plowed up a piece of lead weighing between two and three pounds. John Shew . . . and Jesse Riddle immediately sunk a shaft on the spot, and found ore in paying quantities at a depth of from 15 to 20 feet, which caused a season of wild speculation. . . . It is estimated that within 30 days, 10,000 people came pouring in from all directions, in all conceivable kinds of vehicles, some even coming, like [one] maiden lady, afoot and alone.

Irene G. Stone,
The Lead and Zinc Fields of Kansas, 1902

Lead tailing
Cherokee County

Abandoned lead mine
Cherokee County

Erosion, lead and zinc area near Treece
Cherokee County

Erosion
Cherokee County

We encamped at the upper point of the mouth of the river Kansas; here we remained two days, during which we made the necessary observations, recruited the party, and repaired the boat. The river Kansas takes its rise in the plains between the Arkansas and Platte Rivers, and pursues a course generally east till its junction with the Missouri, which is latitude 38°, 31′, 13″; here it is 340¼ yards wide, though it is wider a short distance above the mouth. The Missouri itself is about 500 yards in width; the point of union is low and subject to inundation . . . , it then rises a little above the high water mark, and continues so as far back as the hills. On the south of the Kansas the hills . . . come within one mile and a half of the river; on the north . . . they do not approach nearer than several miles.

History of the Expedition under the
Command of Captains Lewis and Clark
(1814 edition, vol. 1)

Kansas River between
Manhattan and Topeka
Pottawatomie County

Barge construction
Leavenworth County

Commercial fisherman
Leavenworth County

U.S. Coast Guard buoy crew, Missouri River
Atchison County

Tow boat, Missouri River
Leavenworth County

Coast Guard tender, Missouri River
Atchison County

Perry Reservoir
Jefferson County

South Fork, Republican River,
east of St. Francis
Cheyenne County

In 1871 nearly a million cattle were driven north. Six
hundred thousand came to Abilene alone, while Baxter
Springs and Junction City received half as many. For miles
around the chief shipping points the stock was herded
awaiting a chance to sell or ship. From any knoll could
be seen thousands of sleek beeves, their branching
horns glistening in the sunlight and their herders
watchfully riding in the distance. Several counties of central
Kansas were practically turned into cattle-yards, and it
seemed that the industry would soon absorb the
energies of the entire State.

Charles M. Harger, from
Scribner's Magazine, June 1892

Cattle herd
Russell County

Rancher
Logan County

Cattle drive
Cowley County

My attention is at present particularly turned to the subject
of Winter Wheat. I have labored assiduously to dispel
the fears of the people, relative to the adaptation of our soil
and climate to the culture of wheat . . . . I have
never known a failure in the wheat crop of Kansas, and
I have never known a crop that was not a tolerably
fair one.—Though I have never seen better corn anywhere
than I have seen raised in Kansas, yet I consider wheat
a surer crop than corn, for our winters are generally dry and
moderate, so that wheat is not killed out by either
freezing or drowning; and in the spring it comes to
perfection before the drought sets in.

Richard Mendenhall, a Quaker
Missionary to the Indians, 1846

Wheat combine
Barber County

Custom-cutting crew
Sedgwick County

Antique steam-powered tractor
Wyandotte County

Grain elevators, Holyrood
Ellsworth County

Grain elevators, Lakin
Kearny County

The country here is very different . . .
you can make your fields here as
large as you pleas and it lays most
beautifull. . . . The land lies rooling
on the prary but along the river
it is hilly.

> From a letter written by
> Joseph Oakley,
> January 23, 1856

Spring flowers on the Flint Hills
Wabaunsee County

Flint Hills
Wabaunsee County

Prairie west of Deerhead
Barber County

Grassland
Marion County

We have the frame up, and finished on the outside, of a house containing six rooms, a good cellar, . . . a good cemented cistern, that will hold 100 barrels, the well to come by-and-by, . . . and hay packed against the side to keep the wind from whistling through the crevices between the stones. I love the horses and colt, the cow and calf, . . . and in the cold, unfinished condition of the house, I sometimes think the pleasantest place is among the animals.

Mrs. Mary L. Burt, Clay County, Kansas,
from a letter to a newspaper, January 16, 1869

Farmstead
Decatur County

Farm directory
Kearny County

The drug store was the rendezvous for all the farmers coming to town, for apart from its being also the post-office, it was the only place where "medicine" could be obtained. There was no regular saloon or drinking bar in the place, but every one that wanted a drink went to the drug store, and got a little whiskey "medicinally." . . . Another much frequented place was the general store. . . . Here the loafers congregated in good force, sitting round the roaring, red-hot stove, with their heels high up, and chewing tobacco, talking politics, whittling sticks, and eating crackers and cheese.

Percy G. Ebbutt, from
Emigrant Life in Kansas, 1886

Post office
Johnson County

Country store, Holliday
Johnson County

At last the long-felt want has been supplied at Coldwater, Comanche County,
Kas., in the way of a new paper, the Western Star, with Cash Bros. at the helm.
Politically it is independent. Long may she live and shine to illuminate
the entire country, so as to enable home-seekers in the far west to find their way
through the dark and desolate country.

Columbus, Kansas, *Advocate,*
September 5, 1884

Street scene, Coldwater
Comanche County

There has always been something very interesting to me in the coming of different peoples to Kansas, and the blending of all of them into a community of interest and language. In my newspaper travels I have interviewed a half-dozen varieties of "colonists," among them the Hungarians, of Rawlins county, and the colored folks of Nicodemus, who came to Kansas from the distant and foreign shores of Kentucky.

Noble L. Prentis, from
Kansas Miscellanies, 1889

An eighty-year-old resident of Nicodemus
Graham County

There was no undertaker and no lumber with which to make a
coffin nearer than . . . fifty miles away. . . . We placed the bodies on
the slope of the prairie a little distance from the tent in which
they had died. Samuel and I, with another neighbor, dug
the graves just over a swell of the prairie and out of sight of our
cabin so that the women might not see.

Watson Stewart, pioneer, 1860

Grave near Stull
Douglas County

I had eight years there and it was the best thing that ever happened to me. They taught you more than subjects in that one-room schoolhouse. They taught you about being a person. Maybe it was the Flint Hills here, maybe it was the way we lived. But we learned. We were the lucky ones.

Cecil Horsley, recalling his days at
No. 49 school, Keene, Kansas

One-room school, Stranger Creek valley
Leavenworth County

Children at recess at a one-room school
Leavenworth County

The creeks are all wooded. Fuel would be sufficient for a
considerable population—chiefly elm, cottonwood, and willow near
the rivers—farther from the rivers is more wood on the creeks
and of different kinds.

From the journal of Isaac McCoy,
exploring eastern Kansas, 1830

Wolf Creek
Johnson County

Creek west of Eudora
Douglas County

Stone bridge over a creek
west of Lawrence
Douglas County

The earliest of these peoples apparently came in from the east or northeast, spreading westward up the Kansas River and its branches. Their villages of perishable thatch or bark huts were placed on the small flood-free terraces in or at the mouth of creek valleys tributary to the main river valleys. Their material remains, [and] so far as archeology is concerned, strongly reflects . . . participation in native civilizations once widely distributed in the Ohio and upper Mississippi River valleys. Just how long ago they came, we do not know.

Waldo R. Wedel,
Some Problems of Kansas Prehistory

Carvings by Indians in sandstone above Kanopolis Reservoir
Ellsworth County

In the Smoky Hills of north-central Kansas are Dakota clays and
sandstones, picturesque in their natural form and useful in
the making of bricks. In western Kansas thousands of miles of stone
fence posts may be seen, quarried from the upper strata of the
Greenhorn limestone formation. When first unearthed, this rock
is easily sawed, but hardens when exposed to the air.

Margaret Whittemore, *Historic Kansas:*
A Centenary Sketchbook

Smoky Hill valley
Logan County

Limestone fence posts
Ellsworth County

The territory now comprising our state was carved from the plains sloping eastward from the Rocky Mountains, formerly known as the Great American Desert. I fear that it is still so considered by many untutored people living east of the Allegheny Mountains.

Thomas F. Doran, president of the
Kansas Historical Society, 1937

Mushroom rocks near Carneiro
Ellsworth County

Horse Thief Canyon
Ellsworth County

I almost got lost on the high prairie in the high wild grass. At almost every step one starts up a wild pigeon or a flock of prairie chickens or a covey of quail.

From a letter by Francis Huntington Snow,
September 3, 1866

Blue and snow geese
Atchison County

Little blue herons, Marais des Cygnes River
Linn County

Starling on river piling
Wyandotte County

The very first [troop] trains through Kansas contained men who were most assuredly a very unruly and rough bunch. . . . There were Mormons, Mexicans, Indians, Negroes, businessmen, teachers and construction men. Further, there were drunkards, bootleggers, gamblers and prisoners.

World War I report by the U.S. Railroad
Administration on the first trains of draftees

War veteran
Miami County

What a tragic difference there is between the light which springs from the dawn, and the glow which falls from the sunset.

William Allen White,
from *The Real Issue*, 1896

Sunset
Scott County